UNDERSTANDING
The Whole Counsel of the Kingdom

The Central Message of Jesus and Paul

Frank N. Mitchell

This UNDERSTANDING booklet is part of a series of booklets on key issues of our time on the Reign of Christ at
www.ashiningcityonahill.org
www.reignofchrist.org
All booklets are available at amazon.com

September 2018

Preface

This UNDERSTANDING booklet is one in a series of booklets concerning **THE REIGN OF CHRIST** for our time and how that Reign plays out in all history and as foretold in the Bible.

The problem that I have encountered over the last 30 or 40 years is that Christians who think we should be praying and working for the Kingdom to come on Earth (in order to have the thousand year Reign of Christ in all its fullness) are generally Liberals and apostates who have a false and counterfeit Social Gospel and Social Justice message and understanding of the Kingdom come on Earth and of any possible millennial era of Christ.

On the other hand solid Bible-believing Christians, for a variety of reasons, often tend to be what are called amillennialists and premillennialists, and these folks generally think we are *not* to be praying or working for the Kingdom outside of some minor evangelism and works of charity. Their view is, tragically, that Jesus told us to hunker down in the churches and to wait for Him to return and for this current age to end or the world to end as we know it.

The practical importance of all of this cannot be overstated. It means few if any conservative Bible commentators are really thinking about what it would mean for the Kingdom of God to come on

Earth in all its fullness in the much prophesied worldwide Reign of Christ.

And to further complicate these matters there are many aspects to an actual Kingdom Era come here on planet Earth, and there are many obstacles to how such a Kingdom might well play out in actual history. And, finally, for a true Kingdom come on Earth there are many interrelated political, religious and economic difficulties and confusions in our time to be resolved and overcome.

Given this situation, each booklet in this UNDERSTANDING series tends to stand on its own in order to address some given specific problem or set of problems concerning a coming millennial era on Earth where we will see the nations or "kingdoms of this world become the kingdoms of our Lord and of His Christ."

In this coming time, *each shall know the Lord from the least to the greatest* and *the knowledge of God will fill the whole world as waters cover the sea*. And in this Kingdom time, we will see, worldwide, true worship of God in Spirit and Truth, and we will see all the nations in harmonious interaction in Peace, Justice, and Righteousness.

This will then be the much prophesied and long anticipated reign of the Son of David in a worldwide Reign of Christ.

Frank Mitchell

UNDERSTANDING
The Whole Counsel
of the Kingdom
The Central Message of Jesus and Paul

The Kingdom of God has been correctly defined, in my opinion, by the great Bible teacher J. Vernon McGee who said the Kingdom of God is wherever the Spirit of God reigns. It is well-known that Jesus came preaching the Kingdom of God was at hand as a central unifying point of his ministry on Earth.

What in my experience is not as well-known is that the same is true of Paul. The reason why this is not well-known about Paul is that he only mentions it a few times as the central point of his ministry when he says he is attempting to preach and teach the Kingdom or "the whole counsel" of the Kingdom. (See Acts 20:27 and Acts 28:30-31.)

Paul's Central Message
For whatever the reasons the two particular passages in Acts cited above on the Kingdom of God and "the whole counsel" of the Kingdom of God are not generally commented on at length by most of the great Bible commentators such as Matthew Henry or John Wesley or in the Geneva Bible. In truth, most commentaries do not work out a systematic study of Kingdom teachings even by Jesus, but with Paul

there seems to be an almost total lack of awareness that the Kingdom of God and the whole counsel of it was a central point of Paul's teachings.

The reason for this, I think, is that in chapter two of First Corinthians Paul says he resolved in Corinth to preach nothing but Christ crucified for our sins and, in essence, that would be justification by faith, which is what we most commonly associate with Paul.

However, Paul, in reality, in the passage in First Corinthians about preaching only Christ crucified is not defining his entire ministry as a whole. Rather, he is saying that an **only** "Christ crucified" message is what he resolved to do specifically in Corinth. However, the Corinthian church would come to have many problems of carnality, sin, strife, division, etc., and it is one of the churches Paul would have the most problems with, and so much so that he came to even question their salvation. (See 2 Corinthians 13:5.)

In this context he subsequently goes to the Ephesians, and he says he resolved in Ephesus to preach and teach the Kingdom and the Whole Counsel of it. I use caps here because the Whole Counsel of the Kingdom of God is a specific thing that Paul resolved to teach at some point. In fact, the last verse of the book of Acts says that when Paul was in house arrest in Rome for two whole years that he preached in those two years the Kingdom of God and things concerning Jesus.

This starts to beg the question with Paul every bit as much as with Jesus. What does the Whole of the Kingdom of God entail? To answer this question for both Paul and Jesus, one must use a bit of common sense and one must look at the totality of what both Paul and Jesus taught and then attempt to put it together in a package in order to create a summary statement of the Whole Counsel of the Kingdom of God.

Jesus and the Whole Counsel of the Kingdom
The final charge of Jesus to go into all the world and preach the Good News of salvation in Christ is usually called the Great Commission, but the Great Commission is just part of **the final instruction of Jesus** in the Gospels about what his followers should be about, implicitly in Kingdom work.

In the closing verses of his Gospel, Mark has in the final charge of Jesus to be "baptized" to be "saved" for salvation. And Luke concludes his Gospel with a final charge by Jesus (Luke 24:47) "that repentance and remission of sins should be preached in his name among all nations, beginning at Jerusalem." Each of these passages adds a different element to the whole teaching and instruction of Jesus.

John in his Gospel summarizes the message of Jesus by saying (John 1:12) "as many as received him, to them gave he power to become the sons of God, even to them that believe on his name." Other charges include make disciples, follow me, explain fulfilled prophecy of the Law, Prophets and the Psalms, and teach what I have taught, which would include certainly and even primarily the Two Great Commandments.

Please note, each of these points is a *different* element of the central teachings of Jesus, and when taken all together they tend to make a Whole Counsel of the Kingdom of God by Jesus himself. The problem is that this is too general for a Whole Counsel statement because it includes everything from *all* of fulfilled prophecy to *all* things Jesus taught.

The way to deal with this Whole Counsel question is to look at the **central teachings** of both Jesus and Paul and how those teachings fit together to form a Whole Counsel of the Kingdom of God for each of these men in their particular ministries.

The Christian Cosmology and the Mysteries of Life and Existence
There are different ways to approach this Whole Counsel task, but I have found one way that works well is to look at Paul's famous sermon on Mars' Hill in Acts 17 because in that sermon Paul lays out for the Gentile mind the entire Christian cosmology from the Creation to the Final Judgment, and how the life, death, and resurrection of Christ fit into the whole story of the entire creation and the whole story of man on planet Earth.

But even that sermon on Mars' Hill is itself a compressed version of the larger story that is told by Paul in his various letters. What is the story? God created the universe and everything in it, and He created man, and man fell into sin in the Garden of Eden and became separated from God, and therefore, mankind needs the atoning sacrifice of Christ to be reconciled to God **and** to get back the spiritual life that died in Adam the day he ate the forbidden fruit. For the atheist and for the Liberal this is all a bunch of silliness, mythology, and superstition. And both the modern atheist and Liberal feel justified in their views because of the rise of modern science. However, both the modern atheist and the Liberal are mistaken in this.

In truth, modern science does **not** explain many, if not most, of **the mysteries of existence**. This means both the modern atheist and Liberal are delusional and even "ensnared" by literal demonic deception says Paul. (See, for example, 2 Timothy 2:26.)

Modern science says that the universe is **not** infinite and self-existent. This makes for a big problem. The universe had a beginning, whether by a Big Bang or otherwise. Rather obviously the universe did not create itself or Big Bang itself into existence. All the atomic particles of the entire universe were compressed into a ball the size of a pecan and they decided one day to blow themselves up and form a universe! So, no more mystery, foolishly say both the modern atheist and the Liberal.

The same sorts of problems exist for the mystery of life and human life on Earth. Lightening bolts supposedly hit a hot dilute soup and life sprang up, pop! And life slowly evolved into humans by chance, mutation, and survival of the fittest, no problem. And though the fossil record mysteriously lacks any significant transitional species, no more mystery, foolishly say both the modern atheist and the Liberal.

Then there is the mystery of the mind body problem, and there is the mystery of the reality of the spirit of love and hate, etc. These can be easily dealt with by the modern atheist. Just deny heart, mind, and spirit even exist in the first place in order to be a mystery in the second place! Problem solved, no more mystery, foolishly say both the modern materialist atheist and the modern atheist Liberal, yet again, presumably because of demonic deception and ensnarement into total foolishness just to common sense.

In antiquity there were many so-called "mystery religions" that supposedly explained the mysteries of life, but these pagan mystery religions were just explaining things in terms of pagan deities or supposed cosmic metaphysical forces interacting that we have no reason to believe even exist. It is **only** the God of the Bible and the story of the Christian cosmology in the Bible that accurately and reasonably explain all the mysteries of life and existence and that explain the fact that there is a real right and wrong, a real good and evil, and a real sin to separate us from God, who is perfectly Just and Righteous. But, tragically, yet again, both the modern atheist and the Liberal are in total denial about all of this, and presumably again because of demonic deception and ensnarement into total foolishness just to common sense.

Jesus on Demonic Deception and Enslavement
Jesus says reading from the book of Isaiah: "The Spirit of the Lord is upon me, because he hath anointed me to preach the gospel to the poor; he hath sent me to heal the brokenhearted, to preach deliverance to the captives, and recovering of sight to the blind, to set at liberty them that are bruised, To preach the acceptable year of the Lord." If one analyzes this famous passage in Luke 4, it is clearly talking about spiritual matters and spiritual realities, and this is so, even if one has "poor" to mean materially poor as well as spiritually poor, as in "Blessed are the poor in spirit."

"Poor in spirit" as Jesus uses the term is not some anemic spiritual condition, but rather it is not thinking more highly of one's self than one should. Paul also says this in Romans 12:3. "Poor in spirit" is not being proud and full of one's self, as the expression goes. Rather, it is genuine and proper or appropriate humility. And to people with true and right humility, the Good News of the Gospel of

Christ has come. What is that Good News? Jesus died on the Cross for our sins in order to give us new life in the Holy Spirit of God that came at Pentecost for each believer and so that we could be reconciled to God and avoid the Final Judgment. The foolishly proud and boastful in spirit and the arrogant, etc., are not really interested in this Good News.

Further, Jesus is talking in the above passage about "recovering of sight" to the spiritually blind, is he not? It could include the physically blind, but that is not the primary meaning, I think it is fair to say. Clearly, heal the brokenhearted is a spiritual reality, and it is something from God, if anything ever was. And what is "deliverance to the captives"? I think it is safe to say Jesus is not talking about letting people out of prison. He is talking about people who are taken captive by demons, literally, and rather obviously he is talking about demonic deception and enslavement.

However, most of the Jewish people missed all of this because they were looking for the prophesied political messiah to do Justice and Righteousness in leading the nation and, hence, delivering the nation and even the whole world politically as another King David. And, indeed, this is **ultimately** part of the Kingdom of God come on Earth in all its fullness and, hence, part of the Whole Counsel of the Kingdom of God pretty much any way you figure it.

What Scripture teaches is that the Kingdom of God comes on Earth in spiritual reality for the Church and all believers at Pentecost, but the Kingdom of God has not come **in all its fullness** until the nations or "kingdoms of this world have become the kingdoms of our Lord and of his Christ," at which time the nations of this world are administered by Christians in Justice and Righteousness, and that will fulfill the political prophesies of the Reign of Christ on planet Earth. For this to happen it is clearly *not* necessary for Jesus to be here physically in the flesh.

The Whole Counsel of the Kingdom of God
Jesus said in his famous Sermon on the Mount that he did not come to destroy the law but to fulfill it. And he also said elsewhere that *all* the Law of Moses and the Prophets are contained in the Two Great Commandments (of love God with all your heart, mind, and soul, and love your neighbor as yourself).

So, this means the key to understanding the Whole Counsel of the Kingdom of God involves a whole list of things. One needs to understand the Two Great Commandments along with the Christian cosmology from the Creation to the Final Judgment as well as numerous other things such as the atoning, redeeming work of Christ, justification by faith, the broken power of Satan for those in Christ, the coming of the Spirit at Pentecost for the Church and all believers, and the coming of the Kingdom in all its fullness when the nations of this world have become in the spiritual realm the nations of our Lord and of His Christ in Justice and Righteousness, which is, interestingly, specifically and not coincidentally the American founding model.

The Two Great Commandments
But a big question arises here if, as Jesus says, *all* the Law of Moses and the Prophets are contained in the Two Great Commandments. We must ask what is the big deal about the Two Great Commandments for a Whole Counsel of the Kingdom of God?

The first commandment represents a God-based life in love and **the second commandment** represents the **Golden Rule** (Do unto others as you would have them do unto you). The second commandment and the Golden Rule are summary statements of the **Higher Moral Law** (sometimes called the **Natural Law**) as well as practical principles of application of that moral law.

As C. S. Lewis said, once you have an actual **Creator God of Love** and **a real moral good** of God (a moral good which is associated with and even identified with God) everything else tends to fall in place pretty easily. Why? Because then it makes completely good sense to say John 3:16: "For God so loved the world, that he gave his only begotten Son, that whosoever believeth in him should not perish, but have everlasting life." This truth of John 3:16 is not foolishness at all nor is it superstition or mythology, and it makes completely good sense to say as Hebrews 11:6: "...without faith it is impossible to please Him: for he that cometh to God must believe that He is, and that He is a rewarder of them that diligently seek Him."

As Frances Schaeffer said there is really a God who is "there," and He is really perfectly Righteous and Loving, and one can know him in personal spiritual relationship in one's heart with a peace that passes all understanding by accepting the atoning sacrifice of Christ for one's self and signing on to follow Jesus all the days of one's life in a covenant "I do" relationship, as in a marriage vow and commitment to unity and faithfulness.

The coming of the Holy Spirit for all believers
However, there is a larger point here that is sometimes missed by some Bible commentaries and that is how the actual Kingdom of God come on planet Earth relates to the teachings of both Jesus and Paul. Jesus went about saying repent (turn to the moral good life) because the Kingdom is at hand, and it will come in the lifetime of many of those hearing his teachings. However, because many people think Jesus was talking about a political kingdom of some sort, they miss the fact that the Kingdom in the realm of the spirit that Jesus was talking about came at Pentecost, and it came both as a Spiritual reality of God on Earth generally and as a Spiritual reality and spiritual experience of the Holy Spirit of God *in* all believers in their hearts as a, if not the, central point of the faith and of the Kingdom

spiritually speaking. We know from the late first century or early second century treatise "The Teaching of the Apostles" that the early church thought this, but **so did Paul**. How do we know this?

Jesus came and taught about the Kingdom and what it meant to be his follower; this is straightforward enough. However, Jesus was crucified, and the disciples thought it was over for everything that Jesus was about. They thought all was lost until Jesus rose from the dead and explained to the two disciples on the road to Emmaus that the **crucifixion was fulfilling prophecy** in order to bring about the spiritual Kingdom and reality on planet Earth that Jesus had preached in his teachings prior to the crucifixion. And, further, Scripture says if the demons had known the crucifixion was going to break their spiritual power on Earth and bring on the Kingdom, they would not have motivated the corrupt Jewish leadership and the Roman authorities together to crucify Jesus.

All authority in both the heavenly and earthly realms is now given to Christ, but this understanding of the spiritual Kingdom of God and the reality of it and the purpose of the crucifixion and the fulfillment of prophecy only comes on the road to Emmaus *after* the Resurrection. Further, we know that Jesus continued to explain all of this in detail to his disciples for forty days after Passover *after* his Resurrection and *before* his Ascension. At that time Jesus instructs his disciples to go to Jerusalem and to wait for power of the Kingdom from on high, which it does ten days later at Pentecost, and the rest is history.

Paul had a set system for his Kingdom ministry
However, what we also know is that Paul had a set system for preaching his Kingdom ministry, and that system was he would go to Gentiles in various cities and appeal to their natural conscience (not the Law of Moses) that they were sinners and needed a Savior, and those who came under conviction that this was so would accept Christ and start a church. (2 Corinthians 4:2) This is simple enough, and there is nothing complicated here.

However, Paul would *also* go to the synagogues in various cities, and in the synagogues to a Jewish audience Paul would preach Christ and his crucifixion as a fulfillment of the Law and Prophets in order to set up the actual spiritual, not political Kingdom of God on Earth, which Christ in fact did do. If Paul preaches Jesus to the Jews in the synagogues, logically speaking, it follows this would be the point of his ministry. But Scripture says this explicitly regardless.

In short, Paul was openly and explicitly trying to win the Jews into the spiritual reality and experience of the Kingdom in the earthly realm that came as a reality at Pentecost for the Church, and it was a Kingdom come which even the disciples did not understand until Jesus explained it to them in the forty days after his Resurrection. This specifically became the Kingdom ministry of Paul to the Jews, he says himself as in Acts 28:23: "...there came many [Jews] to him into his lodging; to whom he expounded and testified the kingdom of God, persuading them concerning Jesus, both out of the law of Moses, and out of the prophets, from morning till evening."

Any way one figures it, the Kingdom is about the spiritual reality and experience of Jesus in our hearts by way of the Holy Spirit and about the actual spiritual reality of the Kingdom of God come on Earth for the Church as a whole, and it is about the power of Satan being broken on planet Earth for those in Christ and so much so that Satan would never have motivated people to crucify Christ if he had known this loss of power and authority on planet Earth would happen for those in Christ. However, as it is, the whole rest of the world is actually under the sway or influence of demonic spirits, but of course generally people are often unaware of this. (See 1 John 5:18-21)

This means, when and if the whole world comes to Christian salvation, the Kingdom will cover the world as waters cover the sea and each will know the Lord in their hearts from the least to the greatest, and Jesus will have drawn all men to himself, just as he said he would eventually do if he was crucified for the sins of mankind. (John 12:32-33)

We also know, self-evidently, that this Kingdom has not yet come in all the world and in all its fullness, and this self-evident fact is stated outright in Hebrews 2:8. However, Jesus said that the Kingdom will spread through the whole world as yeast spreads through a whole loaf of rising bread.

This prophesied Kingdom come on Earth in all its fullness is when the nations or kingdoms of this world have become the kingdoms of our Lord and of His Christ. And we know that in the fallen and unredeemed world Satan has ultimate control over the nations of this world and that he even offered them to Jesus in a temptation in the desert, if Jesus would bow down and worship him. Jesus would not, famously, but Jesus will get all the nations eventually, say all the political prophesies concerning the Kingdom come on Earth in all its fullness. When and how does this happen?

The Kingdom in all its fullness
Throughout the whole world Christians, who have the literal Spirit of Christ in them, set up Just and Righteous governments with equal rights for all for the good of the whole nation as a commonwealth and with the consent of the governed. This will be the literal, actual Spirit of Christ over the nations, but it will be in and through the saints administering government and passing good legislation in true Wisdom, which is also *of* God and *is* God, says **Proverbs 8 of Wisdom**, who is also the **Logos of John 1** in what is called Logos-Christology. And this

political situation becomes the literal political "Reign of Christ" over all the nations of the world, and then Kingdom-come prophecies in all their fullness will be fulfilled both spiritually in Christian salvation and politically in Just and Righteous governments.

Such is the Whole Counsel of the Kingdom of God. We clearly see the Church transitioning into this more complete and mature Christianity based squarely on Bible texts in the two track ministry of James Kennedy with his evangelism and cultural mandate ministries and in the Seven Mountain ministries. This is also generally true of the New Apostolic Reformation movement, though that movement makes various errors regarding their own inerrancy and regarding dominion theology over other people and not over Satan.

Conclusion: The Whole Counsel of the Kingdom of God includes the Two Great Commandments as the point of the Christian faith, as they are the point of Judaism, but Christianity adds to them an accepting of the atoning work of Christ for one's self personally, and it adds entering into the Holy Spirit reality of the Church and having the Spirit of Christ literally in our hearts that gives a peace and fellowship with God that passes all understanding.

But *also* the fact that the power and authority of Satan was broken at the Cross is part of the Whole Counsel of the Kingdom. Further, the whole

Christian cosmology from the Creation to the Final Judgment that explains all the mysteries of life and existence is *also* part of the Whole Counsel of the Kingdom of God, as is setting up Just and Righteous government when possible to be administered in the literal, actual Spirit and Wisdom of Christ in the saints.

Who is against any and all of this? Generally speaking, *only* the Devil and people who are deceived and ensnared by his demonic hordes. (See the booklet "UNDERSTANDING Spiritual Warfare.")

===

Other booklets on the Reign of Christ in this UNDERSTANDING Series:

UNDERSTANDING Prophecy Fulfillment:
The Great Apostasy, Babylon, Mystery Babylon & the Reign of Christ

This little booklet gives an overview of the central major prophecies concerning the possible soon coming Reign of Christ. Specifically these are the prophecies of the Great Apostasy, Babylon, Mystery Babylon, and the man of lawlessness. These prophecies are seen as fulfilled in the false millennial visions of Marx and of the New World Order of UN Agenda 21 and Agenda 2030 and in the Liberal World Council of Churches.

UNDERSTANDING All Bible Prophecy:
Genesis to Revelation

This booklet holds that all prophecy should be interpreted in terms of the larger story of the Bible and the larger story of the Christian cosmology from the Creation to the Final Judgment, and this is especially the case for the book of Revelation.

UNDERSTANDING Globalism:
What is the "New World Order"?

This booklet looks at what "globalism" is generally and at the related topic of a "New World Order" that actually has *very* specific definitions and formulations that are often not well-known.

UNDERSTANDING Revelation 19:
Victory over One-World Government and One-World Religion

Revelation 19 though very controversial is actually very straightforward. The saints in a Marriage Supper of the Lamb move into a new more mature, intimate, and complete relationship with Christ, and then the saints in Christ and Christ in the saints completely and totally defeat the evils of one-world government and one-world religion. Simple enough when you get right down to it.

UNDERSTANDING Statesmanship
Classical Justice *versus* Social Justice

Probably no two notions are more misunderstood as well as more necessary to understand in our time than classical Justice and Social Justice. This booklet looks at the history of these two terms and how one stands for the Justice of statesmanship for doing the common good and the other for the injustice of special interest groups and wealth redistribution as a false human right for economic equality.

UNDERSTANDING Alternative Political Universes:
The Natural Revelation & Self-Evident Truths

For some folks as Jefferson and the American founders, the Natural Law or so-called Higher Moral Law is a self-evident truth, but for others with a reprobate mind and no common sense, this is not the case at all. These modern-day people who have lost their common sense are just as the ancient Epicureans (atheist hedonists) while modern-day Liberals are just as ancient Gnostics with their false enlightenment and false morality. Understand these things, and you will pretty well understand Alternative Political Universes.

UNDERSTANDING Illegal Immigration:
The Wall and All It Stands For

"The Wall" of Donald Trump stands for many larger issues from exposing hypocrisy among professional politicians to ending globalism, open borders, and the often total lawlessness of our time. Lawlessness of the Liberal and atheist-humanist is, in fact, the spirit of anti-Christ.

UNDERSTANDING The Whole Counsel of the Kingdom:
The Central Message of Jesus and Paul

Both Jesus and Paul preached a Whole Counsel of the Kingdom message, but this is not a generally well-known truth. This booklet looks at the concept of a Whole Counsel of the Kingdom Christianity and what it entails, namely, true worship of God in Spirit and Truth as well as Just and Righteous government.

UNDERSTANDING Spiritual Warfare:
Satan as a Roaring Lion

Scripture tells us that Satan goes about like a roaring lion seeking whom he may devour, but this is generally not a very understood warning, and tragically many people, if not devoured completely, get an arm or leg eaten (so to speak). To be forewarned is to be forearmed. This booklet deals with ways to recognize and deal with demons.

===

All of the above booklets are part of a series on key issues of our time on the Reign of Christ at
www.ashiningcityonahill.org
www.reignofchrist.org

All of the above booklets are put together is a single **Volume I** called

UNDERSTANDING The Reign of CHRIST
The One Big Issue of Our Time
Volume I

This Volume I of all the above booklets together as well as all of the above booklets separately are available at **amazon.com**

www.ingramcontent.com/pod-product-compliance
Lightning Source LLC
Chambersburg PA
CBHW061330250726
48657CB00003B/1108